How do I feel about

BULLIES AND GANGS

Julie Johnson

COPPER BEECH BOOKS • BROOKFIELD, CONNECTICUT

Designed and produced by
Aladdin Books Ltd
28 Percy Street
London W1P OLD

First published in the United States
in 1998 by
Copper Beech Books,
an imprint of
The Millbrook Press
2 Old New Milford Road
Brookfield, Connecticut 06804

Printed in Belgium
5 4 3 2 1

Designer   Tessa Barwick
Editor   Jen Green
Illustrator   Christopher
                  O'Neill
Photographer   Roger Vlitos

**Library of Congress
Cataloging-in-Publication Data**
Johnson, Julie.
Bullies and Gangs / Julie Johnson : illustrated
by Christopher O'Neill.
p. cm. — (How do I feel about)
Includes index.
Summary: Discusses why people bully others,
who they pick, and how to cope with the
problems of being bullied.
Romanized record.
ISBN 0-7613-0807-5 (lib. bdg.)
1. Bullying—Juvenile literature.
[1. Bullying. 2. Bullies.]
I. O'Neill, Christopher, ill. II. Title. III. Series.
BF637.B85J63 1998
302.3'4—dc21
97-41643
CIP AC

Contents

Introduction

Meet Samuel, Amy, Jonathan, and Neetu as they talk about bullying and gangs. Have you ever been bullied? Would you know what to do if you saw someone being bullied? Samuel, Amy, Jonathan, and Neetu know what it is like to be bullied and have some good tips on how to deal with bullying.

I used to bully, but I don't anymore.

AMY

My gang doesn't bully.

JONATHAN

Bullying is really hurtful.

SAMUEL

Bullying is never right.

NEETU

What Is Bullying?

Samuel and Amy are talking about different kinds of bullying. Samuel knows bullying can be about physically hurting someone. Amy says it can also be calling someone rude names or saying horrible things about them. Taking or hurting someone's property can also be bullying. Have any of these ever happened to you?

Bullying isn't just hitting someone.

Calling people names is bullying.

Stealing can be bullying.

Rude names can be hurtful.

◀ *Money Or Else...*

Bullying is something that happens in every school. Some bullies pick on people who are smaller than they are. They may demand your money or belongings, and threaten to hit you if you don't give them what they want. This is wrong, it is stealing.

▶ *Just A Game*

It is good to be part of a group having fun, as long as everyone is enjoying what is going on. But it's not fun if you get hurt, or aren't enjoying the game.

It's not fun if one person is being picked on to give everyone else a good time.

▲ *Scared To Tell*

Some bullies work in gangs. They may make fun of how you look or the clothes you wear.

They may threaten to hurt you if you tell anyone. Bullies rely on people being too scared to say what is going on.

1. Jack picked on Ben in the playground at lunchtime.

2. Ben was too frightened to tell anyone that he was being bullied.

3. Mrs. Thomas saw the boys and came over to see what was happening.

Do you think Jack was just playing?

No. It's not playing if someone scares you, or makes you do anything you don't want to do.

Mrs. Thomas noticed Jack threatening Ben. Bullies pick a place where they think they won't get caught. Bullying can happen in the playground, the school corridors or bathrooms, or outside the school. Bullying can happen at home. Wherever it happens, it is wrong.

They never let me join in.

Is Bullying Always Easy To Spot?

It is easy to spot that bullying is going on if someone is being hit or pushed around. But some kinds of bullying are less obvious. Deliberately leaving someone out of a game, and never letting them join in the fun is bullying too. Some bullies may even try to take your friends away so that it is more difficult to tell anyone what is happening. This kind of bullying can make you feel very lonely.

Watch it! Whoops, did I hurt you?

What do you know about bullying, Amy?

"I used to be in a gang that started bullying. We used to bully younger children and some of the older ones who were easy to pick on.

I joined the gang because they seemed really friendly. Then it was hard not to join in when they picked on others. I didn't feel right about it, but I wanted to be part of the gang."

7

Who Is Bullied?

Jonathan and Samuel are talking about people who get bullied. Jonathan thinks that bullies will pick on anyone they can get away with bullying. Samuel says a bully picked on him because he reacted to being bullied, and got upset. Bullying can happen to anyone, whether you are a boy or a girl, short or tall.

Small people can get bullied.

Tall, confident people can be bullied.

Big Or Small?

Bullies pick on anyone who they think is different from them, whether he or she is a different color or from another culture, thin or fat, rich or poor. But we are all different from each other, in lots of ways. If you are bullied it is not your fault. Bullying is always wrong.

Samuel, have you been bullied?

"When I was little I had a lisp. There was a boy in the year ahead of me at school who was always picking on me. He would follow me around and copy the way I spoke. I began to really hate school, I would pretend that I was ill so I didn't have to go."

Who Bullies and Why?

There are lots of reasons why people bully others. Some people bully because it makes them feel important, others have been bullied themselves. Amy says you can't always tell if someone is a bully. Neetu was bullied by someone who was smaller than she was, so it is not only big people who are bullies.

Some people bully so others will look up to them.

It's not always easy to spot a bully.

Both girls and boys can be bullies.

1. Holly wanted to play with Marsha and her friends.

2. Marsha said Holly had to take Max's lunch money as a test before she joined.

3. Holly bullied Max while Marsha and the gang looked on.

Should Holly have taken the money?

No, it was stealing. There are lots of different types of gangs. Some are fun to be part of.

Other gangs want you to prove that you are tough. They may ask you to bully someone before you can be in the gang.

Some gangs try to make you do things you know are wrong. It is not always easy to say you won't go along with what is happening.

"Shut up and give me your allowance."

"I hate you! You're always pushing me around."

◀ Bullied At Home

Some people start to bully because they are being bullied at home, by a brother, a sister, or by a parent. Adults can be bullies, too.

Some bullies are copying the way they see other people behave.

"At my new school I'll bully first before they bully me."

▶ It's Not Cool To Bully

Some people bully because they think it will win friends and make others admire them. But what sort of friends does a bully really have?

Real friends are people who like being with you and having a good time, not people who are scared of you.

"They'll all think I'm great."

▲ Tit For Tat

If you have been bullied at school, you may feel the only way to stop the bullying is to become a bully too.

But you know what it feels like to be bullied. Do you really want others to feel the same?

Taking It Out On Others

If you have been bullied you may feel angry. You may want to take it out on someone else. But it is never right to pick on others because you have been hurt. Some people bully because they feel jealous of other people or their belongings, or because they feel no one likes them. But bullying is not the answer to any of these things.

Amy, why did you begin to bully?

"My mom and dad never paid much attention to me. They listened to my brother but never me. In the gang I used to bully to get people to notice me and listen to what I said. But my teacher found out about the bullying and spoke to Mom and Dad.

We talked and things got better. I left the gang and found some new friends."

13

What Can Be Done?

Neetu and Jonathan are talking about what can be done to stop bullying. When Jonathan was bullied he told the bully to leave him alone and walked away. Neetu says it's important to tell an adult you trust, too. They will be able to help both the person being bullied and the bully.

1. Paul was always being bullied by Mark. He didn't know what to do about it.

2. Paul's brother said Paul should hit Mark back, but that might make things worse.

3. Paul decided to stand up for himself and tell Mark to leave him alone.

What do you think of Paul's idea?

It is not easy to know what to do when you are being bullied. Some people say hitting back will stop the bullying, but you might get in trouble or be badly hurt. Try telling the bully to leave you alone. Practice in front of a mirror until you feel confident.

When you are bullied, say the words you have practiced clearly and walk away.

1. Laura saw Pete's gang bullying Jim. She felt scared to try to stop them.

2. After school she had a talk with Mrs. Black.

3. Mrs. Black spoke to Pete and found out why he had started to bully others.

Was Laura right to tell?

Yes. It is hard to know what to do if you see someone being bullied. You might feel it has nothing to do with you, or be worried that you might get bullied too if you say anything. Find an adult you trust and tell them what is happening. They will probably be able to stop the bullying without the bully knowing anyone has told.

Getting Help

If you see someone being bullied, think about how you can help them. Don't just stand by and let it continue.

Think how you would feel if it was happening to you.

If you are being bullied, tell an adult. Think carefully about who to tell. It could be your mom or dad, a teacher, or a classroom helper. If the first person you tell does not take you seriously, go on telling until you find someone who will help you.

Leave her alone. Sarah, come and play with us.

Neetu, how can you stop bullying?

"You will need to judge the situation carefully. Fighting back won't help, so stay calm. You might try to ignore the bully. If you don't get upset, the bully might give up. You might stand up to the bully. But if you can't sort it out for yourself, tell an adult. Bullying is never right and bullies need help to stop bullying."

How Do You Feel?

Samuel and Neetu know that when you are bullied you can feel angry or frightened, lonely, hurt, miserable, or just confused. You may not want to eat anything. You may not be able to sleep, or you might have nightmares. When Samuel was bullied he couldn't face school.

Being bullied can make you angry.

Bullies can make you upset.

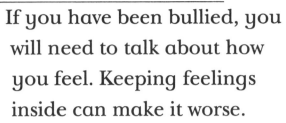

Don't worry. It'll be OK.

▶ It's Good To Talk

If you have been bullied, you will need to talk about how you feel. Keeping feelings inside can make it worse.

Think about who you can talk to easily. It might be your friend, your mom or dad, sister, brother, or another adult.

▲ Feeling Good

When you are being bullied, try to remember it is not your fault. The bully may have picked on something about you that is different, as an excuse to bully you. But everyone is different. Think about the good things about yourself and what you do well.

Samuel, did you talk to anyone?

"I didn't tell anyone about the bullying for a long time. I was miserable and scared, and I thought no one could help.

Mom asked me what was wrong, and spoke to the principal of my school. He talked to the bully and the bullying stopped."

Gangs

Jonathan and Amy both belong to a gang. Most gangs are
about friends being together, having a good time and doing
the things they like. But Jonathan's old gang put pressure on
him to do things that he felt were wrong. It's not good to be
part of that kind of gang.

Gangs Can Be Great!

It can be good to be part of a gang. It feels great to know that your friends are behind you, and support you whether you win or lose.

But it may be hard not to go along with what the gang is doing if you disagree. You may feel you will lose your friends if you won't be part of what is happening. But in the end you have to stand up for what you think is right.

Don't worry, you ran a great race!

My gang really gets things done!

Jonathan, is your gang fun?

"It's super. Paul and I used to be in a different gang but they started bullying. We didn't feel right about it, so we left the gang and started our own. The bullies were annoyed but we kept out of their way and soon they stopped bothering us."

Don't Forget . . .

Samuel, how did it feel to be bullied?

"It's really horrible to be bullied. When you are being bullied it may be difficult to believe that it can ever stop.

But bullying can only go on if the person being bullied keeps quiet about it. Tell an adult you trust. Tell your friends how you are feeling, too. Some people think bullying is part of growing up. But no one should put up with bullying."

What does your gang do, Jonathan?

"We do lots of things — swimming, football, trips to the movies. We look out for each other. Paul had a great idea when we started the gang. Instead of bullying, we would watch out for people who were being bullied. If we see someone being bullied, we tell the bully to stop. If it's a gang we tell an adult who will help sort it out."

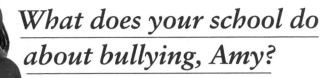

What does your school do about bullying, Amy?

"At my school we had a class discussion about bullying. We talked about what it felt like to be bullied and the bullies said how they were feeling too. Bullies need help to think about other people's feelings as well as their own. They need to understand how their actions affect other people.

Whatever the reason, it is always wrong to bully."

NO!!!

Neetu, what are your tips for dealing with bullies?

"It's not easy to know what to do about bullying. Sometimes it's possible to stand up for yourself. Practice in front of a mirror first. If that doesn't work, tell a grown-up who can help. Don't be scared of telling, it is often the bravest thing to do."

23

Index

All the photographs in this book have been posed by models. The publishers would like to thank them all.